HUCKLEBERRY COOKBOOK

HUCKLEBERRY COOKBOOK

Alex and Stephanie Hester

ThreeForks®

GUILFORD, CONNECTICUT
HELENA, MONTANA

AN IMPRINT OF THE GLOBE PEQUOT PRESS

To buy books in quantity for corporate use
or incentives, call **(800) 962–0973**
or e-mail **premiums@GlobePequot.com**.

ThreeForks is a registered trademark of Morris Book Publishing, LLC.

Illustrations by Robin Ouellette, copyright © 2008 by Morris Book Publishing, LLC

Text design by Sheryl P. Kober

Library of Congress Cataloging-in-Publication Data
  Huckleberry cookbook / Alex and Stephanie Hester.
    p. cm.
  Includes index.
  ISBN: 978-0-7627-4795-5
  1. Cookery (Huckleberries) I. Hester, Stephanie. II. Title.
  TX813.H83H47 2008
  641.6'4732—dc22   2008011487

Printed in the United States of America
10 9 8 7 6 5 4 3 2 1

To Jack

CONTENTS

INTRODUCTION

Like grizzly bears, glistening glacial-fed streams, and snow-capped mountaintops, huckleberries are an iconic western symbol—one that conjures up visions of pure wildness. They are one of nature's true delicacies, and in the West the wild huckleberry is prized among all other berries.

Wild is just one word to describe the huckleberry. It has also been described as a distinctive, elusive, and erratic berry. Distinctive because of its exclusivity; elusive because of its resistance to domestication and its preference for remote environments; and erratic because of its unpredictable yearly production. And like prime picking spots, huckleberries are often described as secretive. Much of the information that exists about huckleberries is based on legend and lore, but other particulars do exist including scientific taxonomy and historical records.

Henry David Thoreau was the first to comprehensively study the history of the huckleberry. His earliest findings trace back to 1615 when explorer Samuel de Champlain observed how Native Americans used the berry. Later, the Lewis and Clark journals documented Native American traditions of harvesting, drying, and preparing huckleberries, as well as where they encountered the berry on their expedition. On April 12, 1806, Captain William Clark wrote:

> *The Indians left us about 6 PM and returned to their Village on the opposit Side. mountains are high on each Side and Covered with Snow for about ⅓ of the way down. the growth is principally fir and White Cedar. the bottoms and low Situations is Covered with a variety Such as Cotton, large leafed ash, Sweet willow a Species of beech, alder, white thorn, cherry of a Small Speces, Servis berry bushes, Huckleberries bushes, a Speces of Lorel &c. &c. I saw a turkey buzzard which is the 3rd which I have Seen west of the rocky mountains.*

Traditional native uses for huckleberries included making dyes, making teas for medicinal purposes, mixing them with meat to make a winter staple called "pemmican," mashing the berries and drying them in the sun to make cakes, and celebrating and honoring the berry in ceremonial rituals. With few native fruits, huckleberries were an important nutritional food source not only to natives but also to early settlers in the West throughout the nineteenth century.

In the early twentieth century western settlers began to recognize the economic value of huckleberries, and in addition to household use, they began to sell fresh and canned berries. During huckleberry season, families would travel high in the mountains to harvest berries. Although the primary purpose of these "working vacations" was to pick enough berries to last throughout the winter, extras were picked and sold for profit.

By the mid-1920s, the once uncompromised berry was transformed into a large-scale commercial industry. Technological advances in food preservation (specifically canning), the availability of workers because of the shortage of jobs available during the Great Depression, and the development of forest service roads were all factors that precipitated the rapid growth in commercial huckleberry harvesting. Hundreds of eager pickers flocked to huckleberry camps during the 1930s, particularly in the area of northern Montana where huckleberries were abundant due to the fires of 1910 that created prime growing conditions. Specialized harvesting tools were developed to maximize commercial harvesting.

In 1937, regulation of the huckleberry industry was first insti-
gated.

In the 1940s economic conditions improved and the commercial huckleberry camps began to decline. By 1950, the camps
were a thing of the past and labor shifted to the timber industry.
Since the 1980s there has been a resurgence in the use of huckleberries as a regional product for the tourism market. Today,
one can easily purchase a multitude of huckleberry goods from
jams and syrups to lotions and soaps.

Huckleberry production has been low in recent years, and
many believe the huckleberry has been overexploited at the
expense of damaged plants and food shortages for wildlife. Like
blueberries, huckleberries contain high levels of antioxidants.
This additional draw to the huckleberry may increase market
demand in coming years. Land managers are taxed with the
responsibility of balancing economic and cultural uses of the
huckleberry.

● ● ●

The *Huckleberry Cookbook* goes beyond customary huckleberry fare. Sidebars explore different aspects of the berry, and although we've included a handful of traditional recipes— including jam, pancakes, and pie—we've incorporated the huckleberry in a variety of our favorite dishes and cuisine. Some recipes bring out the full flavor of the huckleberry while others utilize its flavor to complement or accent the other main ingredients. The truth is, huckleberries can accompany most anything.

Although nothing could ever replace the huckleberry, blueberries are a good substitute for virtually any of the recipes included in this book. So if it's the middle of winter, and you've depleted your huckleberry supply, you won't have to wait until summer to create the flavorful cuisine in this book.

Simply put: Huckleberries are a treat. They are the essence of wildness in nature. Not sweet, not sour, they embody the perfect balance of flavor to scintillate the palate. This book contains an abundance of recipes to enjoy huckleberries in a variety of ways. But perhaps our favorite recipe happens to be the easiest to prepare; that's the field-dressed huckleberry—fresh and au naturál.

Breakfast and Brunch

HUCKLEBERRY SOUR CREAM COFFEE CAKE

We love this coffee cake and have made it with a variety of berries including a mixture of blueberries, blackberries, and huckleberries. It is best served fresh.

Batter
2 cups all-purpose flour
2 teaspoons baking powder
1 teaspoon baking soda
8 tablespoons (1 stick) unsalted butter,
        room temperature
¾ cup granulated sugar
1 ½ teaspoons vanilla
3 eggs
2 cups sour cream
2 cups huckleberries

Crumble Topping

¼ cup brown sugar, firmly packed

¼ cup all-purpose flour

½ teaspoon cinnamon

2 tablespoons unsalted butter, room temperature

Prepare a 9-inch spring form pan or round cake pan with cooking spray or butter and flour. Combine the flour, baking powder, and baking soda together in a mixing bowl. Set aside. In a separate bowl, cream the butter, sugar, and vanilla. One at a time, add the eggs until mixture is smooth and thoroughly mixed. Add dry ingredients to butter mixture without overmixing. Fold in sour cream.

In prepared pan spread half of the batter. Layer the huckleberries on top. Spread remaining batter on top of the berries. Set aside and prepare crumble topping.

Blend brown sugar, flour, cinnamon, and butter with a fork or fingertips until well mixed and resembles course meal. Crumble mixture evenly on top layer of batter.

Bake at 350°F for 30 to 40 minutes until knife inserted in center comes out clean. Cool and remove from pan.

Serves 8–12

Gingerbread Huckleberry Pancakes

The basis for this recipe came from a relative from Austin, Texas. It's a family favorite. Our huckleberry version adds a new dimension. For a healthy twist, you can combine flour with white, whole wheat, rye, oat, or buckwheat flours.

2 eggs
2 cups flour
2 tablespoons sugar
2 teaspoons baking powder
1 teaspoon baking soda
½ teaspoon salt
¼ cup oil
1¾ cup buttermilk
½ teaspoon ginger
¼ cup light molasses
1 cup huckleberries

Separate the egg yolks from the whites. With an electric mixer whip whites until stiff. In a separate bowl combine flour, sugar, baking powder, baking soda, and salt. Mix in oil, buttermilk, ginger, and molasses until well blended. Fold in whipped egg whites and then huckleberries. Butter or spray griddle or large frying pan. Cook over medium heat until both sides are golden brown and center is cooked.

Makes about 18 pancakes

HUCKLEBERRY BUTTERMILK PANCAKES

These are wonderfully light and fluffy pancakes. Top with huckleberry coulis (pg. 96), huckleberry compote (pg. 97), or your favorite topping.

2½ cups all purpose flour

¼ cup sugar

2 teaspoons baking powder

2 teaspoons baking soda

1 teaspoon salt

2 cups buttermilk

2 cups sour cream

2 large eggs

4 teaspoons vanilla extract

2 cups huckleberries

 Tip: *No buttermilk in the fridge? You can make your own quick and easy. Add one tablespoon vinegar or lemon juice to one cup of milk. Let sit for 10 minutes. Substitute this soured milk for buttermilk.*

In a large mixing bowl combine flour, sugar, baking powder, baking soda, and salt. In a separate small mixing bowl, whisk together buttermilk, sour cream, eggs, and vanilla. Add to dry ingredients. Stir until ingredients are just mixed, making sure not to overmix. Fold in huckleberries. Butter or spray griddle or large frying pan. Cook over medium heat, several minutes per side until golden brown and cooked through.

Makes about 20 pancakes

HUCKLEBERRY BANANA SMOOTHIE

For an even healthier and protein-packed drink, add 1 serving of whey protein powder, 1 tablespoon flaxseed oil, and substitute soy milk for cow's milk.

1 banana, ripe
¾ cup huckleberries
¼ cup vanilla yogurt
¾ cup milk
½ cup crushed ice
Dash of cinnamon

Combine all ingredients in a blender and puree until smooth.

Makes 1 large serving

Species and Identification

Depending on the source, thirty-five to forty species of huckle-berries exist in North America. Related to the blueberry and the cranberry, the huckleberry belongs to the genus Vaccinium *and can be found in remote areas of Washington, Oregon, Idaho, Montana, and British Columbia. Most huckleberry connoisseurs agree that the tastiest species are globe (or blue) huckleberries (*Vaccinium globulare*) and mountain (or big) huckleberries (*Vaccinium membranaceum*).*

 *Is it a huckleberry, hurtleberry, blue-berry, bilberry, dewberry, or whortle-berry? The huckleberry has been called by many names and is often misiden-tified and most often mistaken for the blueberry. However, there are several features that distinguish the huckleberry from all others. To the connoisseur, taste is the predominant distinction. Although passionate blueberry lovers will likely disagree, "blah!" is what many people say when they compare the taste of a blueberry to a huckleberry. The flavor of the huckleberry has endless complexity, whereas blueberries are comparatively plain.*

Depending on the species, huckleberry bushes grow any-where from one and a half feet to five feet tall and have brown or light green branches. The green leaves of a huckle-berry bush are oval shaped and about two and a half inches long. Huckleberry blossoms are bell shaped and usually a whitish pink color. The berries vary in color from purples and deep purplish-blacks to blues and reds. Typically about

the size of a pea, they have smooth skin and a depression at the tip where the flower was. Blueberries tend to be larger and have a more pronounced, scalloped depression. Huckleberries tend to grow widely separated on the plant, whereas blueberries grow in clumps. With a wonderfully pungent smell, the odor of huckleberries is so strong it can permeate through plastic bags. (As such, double bagging is recommended when freezing.) Some pickers claim to find productive huckleberry patches by simply following the aromatic scent of the huckleberry.

If you are hunting huckleberries for the first time, we suggest that you obtain a field guide that identifies and describes the specific species in the area you will be foraging.

● ● ●

Bread Pudding with Huckleberry Compote

This is definitely an indulgent breakfast, but you can serve this anytime of the day. It's particularly tasty in the afternoon with a good, strong cup of tea or coffee.

4 cups day-old bread, cut into 1-inch cubes
¼ cup walnuts, chopped
4 eggs
1 cup brown sugar, packed
2½ cups milk
2 tablespoons vanilla
2 tablespoons cinnamon
¼ cup unsalted butter, melted
Huckleberry compote (pg. 97)

Prepare a 13- by 9- by 2-inch baking pan with cooking spray or butter and flour. Place bread and walnuts in a prepared dish. In an electric blender combine eggs, sugar, milk, vanilla, cinnamon, and butter. Blend well. Pour mixture over bread and walnuts. Cover and refrigerate for up to 24 hours. When ready to bake, preheat oven to 350°F. Bake for 50 minutes or until center is firm. Let stand for 10 minutes. Serve warm with huckleberry compote.

Serves 6–8

BERRY YOGURT PARFAIT

I prefer this dish with vanilla yogurt, but choose your favorite flavor. You can also substitute granola for shredded wheat, grape nuts, or any other crunchy cereal. Use whatever berries you have on hand or prepare with Zested Berry Medley (Pg. 48).

1 cup vanilla yogurt
½ cup of your favorite granola
¼ cup huckleberries
¼ cup blueberries
¼ cup strawberries

Layer all ingredients in a parfait glass or other tall glass and enjoy.

Makes 1 serving

HUCKLEBERRY STRATA

Bursting with rich flavor, this is a great dish for Sunday brunch. It's quick to make and can be prepared up to 24 hours in advance.

2½ cups huckleberries
1 cup huckleberry preserves
8 eggs
2½ cups milk
6 teaspoons unsalted butter, melted
¼ cup maple syrup
1 tablespoon almond extract
1 teaspoon cinnamon
1 teaspoon nutmeg
½ teaspoon ginger
6 large croissants, cut in half lengthwise
1 (8 oz. package) cream cheese, cut into ½-inch cubes
1 cup toasted almonds

Prepare a 13- by 9- by 2-inch baking pan with cooking spray or butter and flour. In a heavy saucepan combine huckleberries and preserves. Heat on low until well mixed for about 10 minutes. Set aside.

In an electric blender combine eggs, milk, butter, syrup, almond extract, and spices. Blend until mixture is frothy. Set aside.

Layer 6 croissant halves in prepared dish. Evenly distribute cream cheese cubes over the croissants. Pour blueberry mixture over the cream cheese. Top with another layer of croissants. Pour egg mixture evenly over the croissants. Using a spatula or spoon, gently press on croissants to moisten. Cover and refrigerate.

When ready to bake, preheat oven to 325°F. Place on center rack in oven and bake for 35 to 40 minutes or until top is golden brown and egg mixture is set. Remove and let stand for 10 minutes. Top with almonds.

Serves 8–12

Breads, Muffins, and Pastries

Huckleberry Bread

Delicious any season, this bread is a good comfort food in the fall and winter. Remember to freeze berries to make a loaf or two when huckleberries aren't in season. Or prepare in summer and freeze a loaf for later.

2 cups all-purpose flour
¾ cup sugar
3 teaspoons baking powder
¼ teaspoon salt
2 eggs
1 cup whole milk
1 teaspoon vanilla
3 tablespoons vegetable oil
1 cup huckleberries
½ cup chopped walnuts or pecans (optional)

Preheat oven to 350°F. Prepare a 9-inch loaf pan with cooking spray or butter and flour. Combine flour, sugar, baking powder, and salt in a large mixing bowl. In a separate bowl whisk eggs and then add milk, vanilla, and oil. Add egg mixture to dry ingredients without overmixing. Fold in huckleberries and nuts. Pour batter into pan. Bake for one hour or until inserted knife pulls out clean. Cool and remove from pan.

Makes 1 loaf

Huckleberry Banana Bread

This is a moist, delicious banana bread and the addition of huckleberries gives it a distinctive, fresh taste.

⅓ cup butter
1 cup sugar
2 eggs
½ teaspoon vanilla
1½ cups all-purpose flour
1 teaspoon baking soda
1 teaspoon salt
4 ripe bananas, mashed
½ cup huckleberries
½ cup chopped almonds (optional)

Preheat oven to 350°F. Prepare a 9-inch loaf pan with cooking spray or butter and flour. With an electric mixer cream butter and sugar. Mix in eggs and vanilla. Next, add flour, baking soda, and salt. Mix well. Add bananas and mix until all ingredients are well blended. Fold in huckleberries and almonds. Pour into prepared loaf pan. Bake 1 hour or until inserted knife pulls out clean. Remove from pan and cool.

Makes 1 loaf

Huckleberry Season

Huckleberry season is relatively brief—far too brief for those who patiently wait for them each summer and who miscalculated their needs the previous year. In general, the first berries begin to ripen in late July and flourish through the beginning of September. A host of conditions including climatic variations, altitude, location, and species dictate the length of the season each year as well as the production. In some years a bush will produce only a couple of cups of berries and in other years a gallon of berries can be collected from the same bush.

During the season, huckleberries are available at farmers markets across the West. Some of these sellers may be using commercial harvesting techniques that are ecologically unsound, so check with your local marketer about their picking philosophy.

Huckleberry Lemon Scones

Like the traditional British scone, these are not particularly sweet. To satisfy a sweet tooth, you can coat all sides with raw sugar before baking rather than just sprinkling sugar on the top.

3 cups all-purpose flour

⅓ cup sugar

2½ teaspoons baking powder

1 teaspoon salt

½ teaspoon baking soda

1 tablespoon freshly grated lemon zest

¾ cup (1½ sticks) unsalted butter, chilled
       and cut into ½-inch cubes

¾ cup huckleberries

1 cup buttermilk

3 tablespoons raw sugar

Preheat oven to 400°F. In a large mixing bowl combine flour, sugar, baking powder, salt, and baking soda. Mix in lemon zest. Add butter. Mix ingredients with pastry cutter or fingertips until mixture resembles coarse meal. Carefully mix in huckleberries. Gradually add buttermilk, tossing with fork until moist clumps form. Do not overmix.

Transfer dough to a lightly floured work surface. Softly knead to bind dough, only about 4 turns. Form dough into 1-inch-thick log. Cut log in a "V" pattern making about 12 wedges. Sprinkle tops with sugar. Transfer to a baking sheet, spacing evenly. Bake about 18–20 minutes or until tops of scones are golden brown. Cool and remove.

Makes 12 scones

Healthy Huckleberry Banana Muffins

These may be healthier than your average muffin, but they are just as satisfying.

1½ cups whole-wheat flour

¼ cup oat bran

½ cup sugar

2 teaspoons baking powder

½ teaspoon salt

3 ripe bananas, mashed

½ cup soy milk

1 egg

2 tablespoons vegetable oil

2 teaspoons lemon juice

1 cup huckleberries

Preheat oven to 400°F. Prepare muffin tins with paper liners or coat with cooking spray. In a medium-mixing bowl, combine flour, oat bran, sugar, baking powder, and salt. In a separate

large mixing bowl, combine bananas, soy milk, egg, oil, and lemon juice. Add dry ingredients without overmixing. Fold in huckleberries. Fill muffin tins about ⅔ full. Bake 20 minutes or until inserted knife pulls out clean. Remove from pan and cool.

Makes 12 muffins

HUCKLEBERRY CORN MUFFINS

Hearty and just barely sweet, this muffin can accompany either your breakfast cereal or a bowl of chili.

1½ cups all-purpose flour
½ cup whole wheat flour
½ cup cornmeal
¾ cup sugar
2½ teaspoons baking powder
½ teaspoon baking soda
½ teaspoon salt
½ cup buttermilk
½ cup orange juice
¼ cup unsalted butter, melted
1 egg, beaten
1 tablespoon freshly grated orange zest
2 cups huckleberries

Preheat oven to 400°F. Prepare muffin tins with paper liners or coat with cooking spray. In a large bowl, combine flours, cornmeal, sugar, baking powder, baking soda, and salt. In a separate bowl whisk buttermilk, orange juice, butter, egg, and zest. Add to dry ingredients, mixing until just moist. Fold in huckleberries. Spoon into prepared muffin cups, filling about ⅔ full. Bake for 20 to 25 minutes or until inserted knife pulls out clean.

Makes 18 muffins

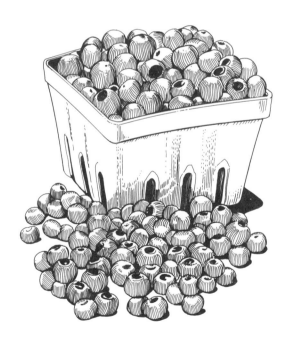

Huckleberry Soda Bread

Here's a nod to our Irish heritage. Typically prepared with raisins, dried berries, or dried fruit, huckleberries update this traditional Irish quick bread and add a new dimension to an old favorite.

2 cups all-purpose flour

2 tablespoons sugar

2 teaspoons baking powder

¼ teaspoon baking soda

¼ teaspoon sea salt

1 cup buttermilk

¼ cup vegetable oil

½ cup huckleberries

3 tablespoons unsalted butter, melted

Preheat oven to 375°F. Prepare an 8-inch bake pan with cooking spray or butter and flour. In a medium mixing bowl combine flour, sugar, baking powder, baking soda, and salt. Add buttermilk and oil, until just mixed. Fold in huckleberries.

Transfer dough to a lightly floured work surface. Softly knead to bind dough, only a couple of turns. Shape into a 6-inch round and place in a prepared pan. With a knife score top of dough with an "X." Place on center rack in oven and bake for 40 minutes or until top is golden brown. Remove from oven and generously brush with melted butter. Best served warm.

Makes 1 loaf

HUCKLEBERRY BEIGNETS

*We fell in love with these deep-fried fritters on a trip
to New Orleans. In this version the Big Easy meets the
Rocky Mountains in an indulgent, scrumptious treat.*

2 eggs
1½ cups all-purpose flour
¾ cup milk
1 tablespoon sugar
1 teaspoon baking powder
¼ teaspoon salt
1 cup huckleberries
Vegetable oil
½ cup powdered sugar

In a large mixing bowl whisk eggs until light and fluffy. Add flour, milk, sugar, baking powder, and salt. Whisk well, making a smooth batter. Fold in huckleberries.

Fill a large deep pot or electric deep fryer with vegetable oil, about halfway up. Heat on high to 360°F.

Gently drop about 6 heaping tablespoons of batter into the hot oil. Be careful not to overcrowd the pot. Fry and turn until beignets are evenly brown on all sides. Remove from oil and place on paper towel. Sprinkle with powdered sugar. Best served warm.

Makes about 20 beignets

Huckleberry Cream Cheese Tartlets

The key to making these pastries look as good as they taste is to work quickly and carefully with the phyllo dough and to crimp the edges together decoratively and firmly so the filling doesn't leak out.

8 sheets phyllo dough
2 tablespoons sugar
4 tablespoons melted butter
4 tablespoons light huckleberry preserves

Filling
8 ounces (1 package) cream cheese
6 tablespoons sugar
1 tablespoon freshly grated lemon zest
1 egg
Huckleberry Compote (pg. 97)

Preheat oven to 350°F. Place two stack of four phyllo sheets each on a flat work surface. Fold one stack lightly in half and brush bottom sheet with butter and sprinkle with sugar. Peel back the next half sheet and repeat. Repeat process on the third half sheet. Do not butter and sugar the top layer. Repeat process on the other side and then with the second stack. Spread top layer of both stacks with preserves. Cut each stack into four squares.

Whisk together cream cheese, sugar, zest, and egg. Place approximately one tablespoon of cheese mixture in the center of each square. Place one tablespoon of compote on top of cheese. Pull up all four corners of the phyllo dough and twist together, forming a free-form cup.

Bake for 12 to 15 minutes or until phyllo is browned and crispy. Cool and serve.

Makes 8 tartlets

Appetizers, Salads, and Sides

Huckleberry Dragon Wings

Spicy with a hint of sweet, these aren't your ordinary wings.

Dragon Sauce

¼ cup soy sauce

2 tablespoons rice wine vinegar

1 tablespoon sesame oil

1 clove garlic

1 tablespoon fresh ginger

1 tablespoon sambal (fresh-ground chili paste)

¼ cup fresh huckleberries

Chicken Wings

2 pounds whole chicken wings

Oil for frying, canola or peanut

½ cup green onions sliced

2 tablespoons toasted sesame seeds

Prepare sauce by placing all sauce ingredients into a blender. Puree until smooth. Pour into a small saucepan and heat through, reducing the sauce slightly. Set aside.

Separate wings by chopping into sections at joints. Discard wing tips. Rinse and pat dry.

Heat oil in a deep pot, to prevent splattering. Bring oil to 360°F. Fry wings in batches for 12–15 minutes or until golden brown. Remove from oil and place on a paper-towel lined baking sheet to drain excess oil. Transfer wings to a bowl and toss with sauce. Place on a platter and garnish with green onions and toasted sesame seeds. Serve hot and cold.

Serves 6–8

BAKED BRIE EN CROUTE
WITH HUCKLEBERRY CHUTNEY

Fresh out of the oven, baked Brie is a succulent hors d'oeuvre—especially when accompanied by this savory huckleberry chutney.

    1 (6-inch) round of Brie
    5 sheets phyllo dough
    4 tablespoons butter, melted
    Huckleberry Chutney (pg. 104)

Preheat oven to 350°F. Place a stack of five phyllo sheets each on a flat work surface. Fold lightly in half and brush bottom sheet with butter. Peel back the next half sheet and repeat until reaching the top layer. Repeat process on the other side.

Once each layer is buttered, place the Brie on the center of the stack of phyllo. Pull up the edges of the phyllo around the Brie and seal. Brush with butter, turn over, and transfer to a baking sheet. Brush the top with remaining butter. Bake for 15–20 minutes or until golden. Place onto a serving platter and garnish with chutney. Serve with crackers or sliced French bread.

Serves 10

ROAST BEEF WITH HUCKLEBERRY HORSERADISH ON CROSTINI

This is a versatile hors d'oeuvre for almost any occasion.

Crostini
1 baguette
¼ cup olive oil
4 cloves garlic, peeled and halved

Topping
½ pound deli-sliced roast beef
Huckleberry Horseradish Sauce (pg. 106)
1 bunch chives, finely chopped

Preheat oven to 425°F. Slice French bread into ½-inch rounds. Place rounds on a baking sheet and brush with oil. Rub each piece with cut side of garlic. Bake 5–7 minutes or until golden brown and crispy. Remove from oven and cool.

Place a small amount of roast beef on each piece of crostini. Top the roast beef with a small dollop of huckleberry horseradish. Garnish top with chives.

Serves 6–8

TAMING THE WILD HUCKLEBERRY

As of yet, the wild huckleberry has not been domesticated, but not for a lack of trying. Although the idea of having access to huckleberries year 'round is inviting, we hope the technology to cultivate or domesticate the huckleberry is never perfected. Mass production in its non-native environment would diminish the berries' unique character, bold flavor, and individuality. This is precisely what happened to the blueberry when it was domesticated nearly two centuries ago. One can try to take the huckleberry out of the wild, but to maintain its integrity you can't take the wild out of the huckleberry.

Turkey Pinwheels with Huckleberry Cream Cheese

Here's a quick snack or a hearty appetizer for kids and adults alike.

4 large tortillas or wraps
½ cup Huckleberry Cream Cheese Spread (pg. 105)
2 cups mixed greens
½ pound deli-sliced turkey
½ pound thinly sliced cheese

Place tortillas on a flat work surface. Spread approximately 2 tablespoons of cream cheese on each tortilla. Layer approximately ½ cup greens over the cream cheese. Dividing equally among each tortilla, layer turkey and cheese on top of greens. Roll tightly. Slice in 1½- to 2-inch rounds.

Serves 8–10

Vichyssoise with Huckleberry Swirl

This French potato-leek soup is served cold. The potato and huckleberry flavors compliment each other nicely and the contrasting colors present a beautiful swirl. A tasty treat.

Soup
1 tablespoon butter
2 large leeks, coarsely chopped
1 sweet onion, chopped
¾ cup dry white wine
4 medium Yukon russet potatoes, peeled and diced
6 cups chicken broth
4 cloves garlic, whole
½ teaspoon salt
½ teaspoon white pepper
3 cups whole milk

Huckleberry Swirl
1 cup huckleberries
2 tablespoons huckleberry preserves
½ cup heavy cream

Melt the butter in a large stock pot over medium-high heat. Add the leeks and onion and stir for about 5 minutes, or until they are translucent but not yet brown. Add the wine and cook for 2 more minutes. Add the potatoes, broth, and garlic. Bring to a boil, cover, and then reduce heat to medium-low and simmer for 40 minutes. (Adjust heat as required to simmer.) Add the salt and pepper. Let the soup cool.

Once cool, puree the soup in a blender or food processor. Refrigerate for a minimum of 1 hour, but overnight is best.

To prepare Huckleberry Swirl, place huckleberries (reserve ¼ cup for garnish), preserves, and cream in blender. Blend until well mixed and thickened.

Just before serving, add 1 part milk for every 3 parts soup. Blend for 15 seconds to aerate. Serve cold in chilled bowls. Place a dollop of huckleberry mixture onto the soup. Use a knife to decoratively swirl. Add a few fresh berries to garnish.

Serves 10–12

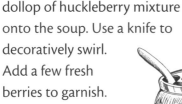

Fresh Fruit Salad with Huckleberry Yogurt Dressing

Give an ordinary fruit salad some extra punch with this wonderful dressing.

Yogurt Dressing
1 cup plain yogurt
¼ cup honey
Juice of 1 lemon
Zest of 1 lemon
½ cup fresh huckleberries
Freshly cracked black pepper

Combine yogurt, honey, lemon, zest, and huckleberries in an electric blender and mix well. Add black pepper to taste. Toss with your favorite combination of fresh fruits.

Makes 1½ cups

WALNUTS, GOAT CHEESE, AND MIXED GREENS WITH HUCKLEBERRY VINAIGRETTE

12 ounces mixed greens
Huckleberry Vinaigrette (pg. 100)
8 ounces goat cheese, crumbled
¼ cup huckleberries
¼ cup walnuts, chopped

Rinse greens and place in a bowl. Toss with dressing. Divide greens among four salad plates. Crumble goat cheese over the greens. Sprinkle with huckleberries and walnuts.

Makes 4 servings

Huckleberry Chicken Salad

Chicken salad is often prepared with grapes or cranberries. We prefer huckleberries, which give this easy-to-prepare salad a fresh, distinctive taste.

2 cups cooked chicken breasts, cubed
½ cup sliced green onion (scallions)
¾ cup diagonally sliced celery
½ cup mayonnaise
1½ tablespoons apple cider vinegar
¼ cup walnuts, chopped
2 teaspoons poppy seeds
1 teaspoon salt
1 cup fresh huckleberries

In a medium bowl combine all ingredients except for berries. Mix thoroughly. Fold in huckleberries. Cover and refrigerate to let flavors blend for at least 30 minutes. Serve over endive or other greens, or in a multigrain wrap.

Serves 4–6

Roasted Potatoes with Thyme and Huckleberries

Huckleberries add a sweet twist to this classic potato dish.

3 tablespoons olive oil

2 teaspoons sea salt

1 teaspoon black pepper

2 teaspoons fresh rosemary

2 pounds potatoes, quartered

1 red pepper, sliced

1 yellow onion, sliced

½ cup fresh huckleberries

Preheat oven to 400°F. In a shallow baking dish mix oil, salt, pepper, and rosemary. Toss potatoes, red pepper, and onion in oil mixture, making sure to coat well. Bake for 40 minutes. Remove from oven, stir, and increase heat to 450°F. Return potatoes to oven and cook for 15 minutes. Sprinkle huckleberries over potatoes and cook for an additional 5 minutes.

Serves 6–8

ZESTED BERRY MEDLEY WITH CHAMBORD

The uses for this mélange are endless ... yogurt, ice cream, pancakes.

1¼ cups (½ pint) huckleberries
1¼ cups (½ pint) blueberries
1¼ cups (½ pint) raspberries
1 teaspoon lemon zest
1 teaspoon orange zest
1 tablespoon chambord (black raspberry liqueur)

Toss ingredients together.

Serves 4

Main Entrees

Huckleberry Glazed Roast Chicken

The huckleberry glaze is a wonderful addition to a freshly roasted, moist chicken. In a pinch, you can whip up the glaze in no time and add to a prepared store-brought roasted chicken.

Glaze
½ cup white vinegar
½ cup unsalted butter
½ cup huckleberries
1 teaspoon granulated sugar
Salt and pepper to taste

Roast Chicken
1 whole chicken (approximately 5 pounds)
¼ cup olive oil
2 garlic cloves, finely chopped
Rosemary sprigs
Salt and pepper

Tip: *Use leftover chicken to prepare Huckleberry Chicken Salad (pg. 46).*

Over medium heat, simmer vinegar and butter in small saucepan. When butter is melted add huckleberries and sugar. Reduce heat to low and simmer for 10 minutes. Remove from heat and let cool. Put sauce in blender or food processor, puree until smooth. Return sauce to pan over low heat to warm. Salt and pepper to taste. Set aside and prepare chicken.

Preheat oven to 400°F. Rinse chicken and pat dry. Place chicken, breast-side up, on rack in a shallow roasting pan. Truss chicken (tie legs to tail).

In a small bowl, whisk olive oil, chopped garlic, and rosemary. Add salt and pepper as desired. Generously coat chicken with mixture.

Place roasting pan on center rack in oven. Roast uncovered for 90 minutes or until thermometer reads 180°F and juice of chicken is no longer pink when thigh is cut. Coat chicken with ⅔ of huckleberry glaze mixture and cook 10 minutes. Remove from oven. Let stand for 15 minutes to reattribute juices.

After carving, spoon remaining huckleberry glaze on chicken for additional flavor and for presentation.

Serves 4–6

PAN-SEARED SALMON WITH HUCKLEBERRY SAUCE

Producing a crispy crust is essential in this dish. The blend of huckleberries and basil are a perfect compliment to the robust flavor of the salmon.

4 salmon fillets
2 tablespoons olive oil
Salt and pepper
⅓ cup water
1 cup fresh huckleberries
1 tablespoon sugar
1 lemon, juiced
¼ cup fresh basil, finely chopped

Heat skillet over high heat. Add olive oil. Salt and pepper both sides of salmon fillets. When pan is hot add fillets, skin side down. Sear for approximately 4 minutes per side. Remove from pan and let rest.

Reduce heat to medium. In the same pan used to fillet fish add water and huckleberries. Simmer until tender. Add sugar and simmer two to three more minutes. Lastly, add lemon juice and basil. Remove from heat and let stand a few minutes. Drizzle sauce over the salmon fillets.

Serves 4

Guide for Huckleberry Hounds

If you are looking for a map that reveals where to find the best huckleberry patches, look no further. One is not supplied in this book, and we're not sure one even exists. Pickers, berriers, or hounds, as they are called, are a private bunch when it comes to huckleberry locations.

Huckleberry picking is a labor-intensive, tedious process. But one that can be very rewarding and enjoyable and provide some solace.

In general, huckleberries are found at subalpine elevations above 3,500 feet on steep slopes and in acidic soils. They are often prolific in burned areas that are ten to twenty years old, grow best in partial shade, and need sufficient moisture.

Huckleberries exist in bear country for bears, although there's enough for us humans too. It's important to be respectful and attentive when foraging for berries. Further, we advocate that zero impact principles be utilized when traveling through the wilderness in pursuit of berries. The delicate ecological balance and future sustainability of the huckleberry are at stake.

We believe hand picking is the only responsible method for collecting huckleberries. During the heyday of huckleberry camps in the 1930s, picking tools were handcrafted including a variety of rakes and bush beaters (literally used to beat the berries off the bush). Although these mechanical harvesting tools increase yields and efficiency, they damage bushes, which leads to lower production in successive years.

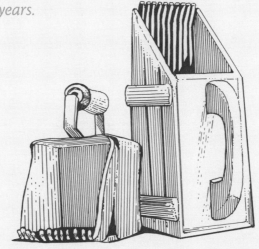

BABY BACK RIBS WITH HUCKLEBERRY BARBECUE SAUCE

This smoky and sweet barbeque sauce can be applied to any grilled meat.

Barbecue Sauce

½ sweet onion, chopped

2 red jalapeños, chopped and seeded

5 cloves garlic, chopped

¼ cup white vinegar

¼ cup molasses

2 tablespoons huckleberry preserves

1 cup ketchup

1 tablespoon dry mustard

1 teaspoon granulated garlic

1 teaspoon granulated onion

1 teaspoon paprika

1 teaspoon fresh ground black pepper

Ribs

2 racks baby back pork ribs

¼ cup sea salt

¼ cup fresh cracked black pepper
¼ cup chili powder
½ cup dark brown sugar

Over medium heat sauté onions, jalapeños, and garlic in a heavy saucepan until soft. Add vinegar, molasses, and huckleberry preserves. Simmer mixture until well incorporated. Remove from heat and add ketchup and dry spices. Use blender or food processor to puree sauce. Refrigerate in covered container and prepare ribs.

Preheat oven to 300°F. Rinse ribs and place bone side down in shallow backing dish. In a small mixing bowl combine salt, pepper, chili powder, and brown sugar. Generously rub ribs with the mixture. Place in oven and cook uncovered for 1 to 1½ hours. Transfer to cutting board to cool for 10 minutes.

Preheat grill to 300°F. Place ribs on aluminum foil bone side down. Smother with prepared barbecue sauce. Place ribs on top rack of grill or other indirect heat source. Grill for 20 minutes or until desired tenderness. Ribs should appear to be a rich golden brown. Let rest before service.

Serves 4

GRILLED PORK TENDERLOIN WITH HUCKLEBERRY CREAM SAUCE

Different cheeses will vary the flavor of this light cream sauce. Fontina is our favorite.

1 – 1 to 2 pound pork tenderloin
2 tablespoons olive oil
1 tablespoon sea salt
2 tablespoons freshly cracked pepper, divided
½ cup chicken broth
⅓ cup half and half
3 tablespoons huckleberries
¼ cup soft cheese (such as
    bleu, goat, or fontina)

Place the pork tenderloin between sheets of wax paper. Tenderize pork by pounding until somewhat flat. Then place in shallow baking dish and rub with olive oil, salt, and half the pepper. Let marinate for at least ten minutes.

Heat a small saucepan over medium-low heat. Whisk half and half with chicken broth, then add huckleberries. Let simmer 5 minutes until sauce is silky in texture. Remove from heat. Immediately add cheese and black pepper to taste.

Place tenderloin on a 400°F grill. Barbecue each side for 10 minutes or to desired doneness. Remove from grill and let rest to allow juices to redistribute. Slice pork and transfer to a serving platter. Drizzle with cream sauce.

Serves 4

PAN-FRIED TROUT WITH HUCKLEBERRY LEMON SAUCE

Through and through this is a regional dish with regional ingredients. The epitome for ultimate freshness is to catch your own trout and pick your own berries.

Sauce

¼ cup fresh huckleberries

2 tablespoons fresh lemon juice

Salt and pepper

Trout and Breading

2 cups flour

½ cup cornmeal

2 tablespoons salt

2 tablespoons ground mustard

2 tablespoons paprika

2 tablespoons granulated garlic

1 tablespoon black pepper

1 teaspoon cayenne pepper

½ teaspoon dried thyme

½ teaspoon dried oregano

2 eggs

½ cup milk

4 trout fillets

½ cup vegetable oil

To prepare sauce combine all sauce ingredients in a blender. Blend until ingredients are incorporated. Set aside and prepare fish.

Combine first ten ingredients in a large resealable plastic bag and shake until well mixed. Set aside.

In a shallow baking dish combine eggs and milk. Dip fish fillets in egg mixture coating both sides. One at a time place the fillets in the plastic bag containing the breading mix and shake until well coated.

Heat the oil in a large frying pan. Transfer fish to pan and cook until golden brown, about 5 minutes per side.

Serves 4

Roast Duck with Huckleberry Hoisin

Huckleberries provide the sweetness in this Chinese barbeque sauce that marries well with the duck.

1 – 4 to 5 pound duck
½ onion
½ lemon

Marinade
2 cups huckleberry wine
½ cup soy sauce
¼ cup natural rice vinegar
2 tablespoons huckleberry preserves
2 tablespoons hoisin sauce
2 tablespoons ginger, peeled and chopped
6 cloves garlic, peeled and smashed
½ onion, chopped
Juice from ½ lemon
2 tablespoons gouchujang (Korean hot pepper paste)
1 teaspoon Chinese five-spice powder
1 teaspoon dry mustard
1 teaspoon ground black pepper

Begin by trimming the excess fat from the duck. Rinse the duck thoroughly, inside and out, and pat dry with paper towels. Place one half of the lemon and one half of the onion in the cavity of the bird. Tie legs together with kitchen twine. Place duck in a large plastic bag.

In a large mixing bowl, whisk together all marinade ingredients. Pour the marinade into the plastic bag and shake, making sure mixture is well distributed. Place bagged duck in a roasting pan. Refrigerate for at least 4 hours or overnight, rotating every so often to distribute marinade. Preheat oven to 375°F. Remove duck from the plastic bag and place on rack in roasting pan, breast side up. Pour marinade from bag into a small saucepan. Place duck on center rack in oven.

While duck is roasting, heat marinade over medium-high heat until it reduces in half. During the roasting process, brush marinade over duck about every 20 minutes. If skin begins to get too browned, tent foil over the duck. Cook for a total of about 2 hours. Internal temperature should reach 180°F. Let sit 10 minutes before carving.

Serves 2–4

Coq Au Huckleberry Vin

Coq Au Vin or "Rooster with Wine" is a classic French dish. Variations abound in France as different regions utilize their own wines and champagnes. Here's our own regional adaptation of this rich and delicious dish.

3 tablespoons olive oil

½ pound thick-cut bacon, diced

1 chicken (about 3 pounds), rinsed and quartered

¾ cup coarsely chopped shallots

2 pounds carrots, peeled and cut into 1-inch lengths

3 tablespoons chopped garlic, chopped

3 tablespoons unsalted butter

2 pounds white mushrooms, cleaned and quartered

3 tablespoons all-purpose flour

2 cups chicken broth

2 cups huckleberry wine

1 tablespoon huckleberry preserves

¼ cup tomato paste

1 tablespoon fresh thyme

1 bay leaf

6 tablespoons parsley, chopped

Egg noodles, prepared per package instructions

Preheat oven to 375°F. In a large Dutch oven, heat oil over medium-high heat on stovetop. Add bacon and render (the cooking process of extracting the fat) until brown and crispy. Transfer to a paper-towel lined bowl. Let sit and drain.

Using the same pot, brown the chicken, about 5 minutes per side. Set aside.

Reduce heat to medium-low. Add shallots and carrots to pot and cook for about 10 minutes or until soft. Add garlic and cook 4 more minutes. Next, add butter and mushrooms and cook 6 minutes. Stir flour into the vegetable mixture and let cook a few more minutes. (This makes the roux or thickener for the sauce.)

Deglaze the pan by adding the chicken broth and huckleberry wine, scraping the bottom to extract the entire flavor. Next add huckleberry preserves, tomato paste, thyme, bay leaf, and salt and pepper. Sample sauce and add salt and/or pepper to taste.

Stir prepared bacon into the mixture. Next add chicken. Spoon sauce mixture over the chicken until it is well coated with the sauce. Bring to a boil. Immediately remove from the heat, cover pot, place in oven, and cook for 35 minutes. Uncover and cook for another 30 minutes. Add parsley and cook for a final 5 minutes. Remove from oven and serve over noodles.

Serves 8–10

GRILLED RIB EYE WITH HUCKLEBERRY CARAMELIZED ONIONS

When prepared, the caramelized onions turn a purplish-blue color, and they taste as good as they look.

1 tablespoon unsalted butter
1 teaspoon olive oil
2 cups sweet onions, thinly sliced
Pinch of salt
½ teaspoon black pepper
½ cup huckleberries

4 rib-eye steaks
Grilling spice of your choice

Combine butter and olive oil in a frying pan. Over medium heat, sauté onions until translucent. Add salt and pepper and cook for 1 minute. Add huckleberries and cook until onions become caramelized (brown and crispy).

Meanwhile preheat your grill to 400°F. Cook rib-eyes to desired doneness. Serve onions atop the steaks.

Serves 4

Desserts

Huckleberry Blueberry Cobbler

Quick and easy, this dish is particularly delicious when served with vanilla ice cream or freshly whipped cream. Mix berries as instructed below, or make with pure huckleberries.

Filling
1 cup huckleberries
1 cup blueberries
1 teaspoon freshly grated lemon zest
⅓ cup sugar
1 tablespoon fresh lemon juice
1 teaspoon cornstarch

Topping
⅔ cup all-purpose flour
1 teaspoon baking powder
¾ teaspoon nutmeg
½ cup heavy cream

Preheat oven to 400°F. Generously butter an 8-inch (1½-quart) glass pie plate. In a medium bowl toss together berries, lemon zest, sugar, lemon juice, and cornstarch until well mixed. Transfer filling to prepared pie plate.

In a medium mixing bowl combine flour, baking powder, and nutmeg. Add cream and stir until mixture begins to form a dough, making sure not to overmix. Drop ¼-cup dollops of dough onto the berry mixture. Bake on center rack in oven for 25 minutes or until topping is golden brown.

Serves 6–8

Bears and Huckleberries

In the Northern Rockies huckleberries constitute an important source of food for grizzlies and black bears. The ripening of the huckleberries coincides with the final feeding stage before the bear's hibernation. Constituting approximately 15 percent of the bear's annual intake, huckleberries are a crucial nutritional element of their diet.

In the West most everyone has heard a story about a berry picker stumbling upon a bear. If you find yourself face-to-face with a bear while picking berries, even if you've found the motherload, it behooves you not to compete with the bear. The bear won't share, so for your safety it's best to back away. There is no evidence that berriers run into bears any more frequently than anyone else. Bears are normally shy and if you stay in groups and make some noise while you are picking, bears are likely to stay away.

There is a precarious balance between people and bears, perhaps especially when it comes to huckleberries. Fortunately, however, bears tend to stick to the higher elevations for their berries while humans tend to stay lower. This helps in maintaining the balance.

HUCKLEBERRY CRUMB CAKE

This is a refreshing dessert served with ice cream, but is also suitable for brunch. Best served freshly baked.

3 cups all-purpose flour

1 cup plus 2 tablespoons sugar

2 teaspoons baking powder

¾ teaspoon baking soda

¾ teaspoon salt

¾ teaspoon cinnamon

¼ teaspoon nutmeg

¾ cup (1½ sticks) plus 2 tablespoons unsalted
     butter, chilled and cut into ½-inch cubes

2 large eggs

1 cup sour cream

2 teaspoons vanilla

3 cups huckleberries

Preheat oven to 375°F. Prepare a 13- by 9- by 2-inch baking pan with cooking spray or butter and flour. In a medium mixing bowl combine flour, 1 cup sugar, baking powder, baking soda, salt, cinnamon, and nutmeg. Mix well with a spoon or whisk. Add ¾ butter. Mix ingredients with fingertips until mixture resembles coarse meal.

Transfer 1½ cups flour mixture to a separate bowl for crumb topping and add remaining 2 tablespoons butter and remaining 2 tablespoons sugar. Blend with your fingertips to form clumps. Set aside.

In a small mixing bowl whisk eggs, sour cream, and vanilla. Add to remaining flour mixture. Stir until mixture forms, making sure not to overmix. Fold in huckleberries. Pour batter into a prepared pan. Evenly sprinkle crumb topping over batter. Bake on center rack of oven for 40 to 45 minutes or until inserted knife pulls out clean. Cool in pan.

Serves 8–12

Huckleberry Crisp

Serve warm á la mode.

¾ cup flour
½ cup sugar
½ teaspoon cinnamon
6 tablespoons (¾ stick) unsalted butter,
    chilled and cut into ½-inch cubes
5 cups huckleberries

Preheat oven to 375°F. Generously butter a 13- by 9- by 2-inch baking dish.

In a medium mixing bowl combine flour, sugar, and cinnamon. With a pastry cutter or fingertips work in the butter until mixture resembles course meal.

Arrange an even layer of huckleberries in a prepared dish. Sprinkle crumb mixture over berries. Bake about 20 minutes or until the top is browned and juices are bubbling.

Serves 6–8

Huckleberry Lemon Trifle

Trifles are labor intensive to prepare but well worth the trouble. Don't worry if you have leftovers; like a good lasagna trifles get better as they age.

Pound Cake
2¾ cup all-purpose flour
1¾ cup sugar
2 teaspoons baking powder
1 teaspoon salt
4 eggs
1 cup butter, melted
1 teaspoon vanilla
¾ cup milk

Huckleberry Sauce
5 cups huckleberries
¾ cup sugar
½ cup water
1 tablespoon fresh lemon juice

Lemon Mousse
8 large egg yolks
1 cup sugar
¾ cup fresh lemon juice (about 3 large lemons)
7 tablespoons unsalted butter, softened and cut
        into ½-inch pieces
1 tablespoon freshly grated lemon zest
1 cup heavy cream

Preheat oven to 375°F. Prepare a 9-inch loaf pan with cooking spray or butter and flour. In a medium mixing bowl combine flour, sugar, baking powder, and salt. In a separate bowl whisk eggs, and then add butter, vanilla, and milk. Add wet ingredients to dry ingredients. Mix completely. Pour batter into prepared pan and bake on center rack in oven for 1 hour to 1 hour 10 minutes or until inserted knife pulls out clean. Cool completely, remove from pan, and cut into 2-inch cubes.

In a small saucepan combine sauce ingredients. (Set aside a handful of berries for garnish.) Simmer on low heat, stirring occasionally, 40 to 45 minutes. Sauce should reduce to about 2½ cups. Remove from heat and cool completely. Cover and chill. May be made up to two days ahead.

To prepare lemon mousse whisk together egg yolks and sugar in a heavy saucepan. Add lemon juice and butter. Cook over moderately low heat, whisking constantly, until butter is completely melted. Continue to cook for approximately 10 more minutes, whisking constantly, until mixture just reaches the boiling point and is thickened. Stir in zest and cool. Cover surface of mixture with plastic wrap and chill for about 2 hours.

Pour cream into a medium mixing bowl. Using an electric mixer beat cream until stiff peaks are formed. Whisk approximately one quarter of the whipped cream into cooled lemon mixture. Gently, fold in remaining whipped cream making sure not to overmix. Cover and chill. Mousse may be made up to two days ahead.

When ready to assemble trifle, arrange one layer of pound-cake cubes on bottom of trifle dish. Spoon ½-cup huckleberry syrup over pound cake. Next, spoon ¼-cup lemon mousse over syrup layer. Repeat layering, ending with mousse layer on top. Carefully cover dish and chill, preferably overnight or for several hours. Before serving, garnish top of trifle with lemon zest and reserved fresh berries.

Serves 8–12

Huckleberry Swirl Cheesecake Bars

Separately, shortbread and cheesecake are rich. Together, they form an intoxicating indulgence. Add huckleberries to that combination and you have something absolutely heavenly.

Shortbread Crust
¾ cup (1½ sticks) unsalted butter, chilled and cut into
    ½-inch pieces
2 cups all-purpose flour
½ cup brown sugar, packed
½ teaspoon salt

Cream Cheese Topping
16 ounces (2 packages) cream cheese, softened
2 eggs
¾ cup sugar
1 teaspoon vanilla
¼ cup huckleberry preserves

Preheat oven to 350°F. In a food processor combine butter, flour, brown sugar, and salt. Process until mixture begins to take shape, forming small lumps. Gently press mixture onto the bottom of a 13- x 9- x 2-inch baking pan until evenly covered. Bake on center rack for 20 minutes or until golden. While baking, prepare cream cheese topping.

In a mixing bowl beat cream cheese with an electric mixer until smooth (about 1 minute). Beat in eggs one at a time. Add sugar and vanilla. Remove ⅓ of the cream cheese mixture and add huckleberry preserves. Poor the plain cream cheese mixture onto the cooled crust. Spoon dollops of huckleberry cream cheese mixture onto the plain cream cheese mixture. Use a knife to swirl the plain and huckleberry mixtures together. Bake on center rack at 350°F for 30 minutes. Cool completely in pan and cut into bars. Refrigerate to store.

Makes 24 bars

HUCKLEBERRY CUPCAKES WITH LEMON CREAM CHEESE FROSTING

Not a berry muffin, these are truly cupcakes. Sweet and light, they are a nice variation of the popular white cupcake.

Cupcakes
5 tablespoons unsalted butter, softened
½ cup sugar
1 large egg
½ teaspoon vanilla
1 cup all-purpose flour
1½ teaspoons baking powder
⅛ teaspoon salt
½ cup whole milk
½ cup frozen huckleberries

Frosting
1 8-ounce package cream cheese, room temperature
2 tablespoons unsalted butter, softened
½ teaspoon vanilla extract
¼ teaspoon freshly grated lemon zest
½ teaspoon lemon juice
½ cup powdered sugar

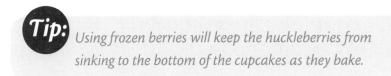

Tip: Using frozen berries will keep the huckleberries from
sinking to the bottom of the cupcakes as they bake.

Preheat oven to 350°F. Prepare muffin tins with paper liners.
In a large mixing bowl add butter and sugar. Beat with an electric mixer for a few minutes until light and fluffy. Add egg and
vanilla. Beat until well mixed.

In a separate bowl sift together flour, baking powder, and
salt. Gradually add dry ingredients to butter mixture, mixing
at low speed, alternating with milk, beginning and ending with
flour mixture. Do not overmix. Fold in huckleberries.

Fill prepared muffin cups about ⅔ full. Bake on center rack
in oven about 20 to 25 minutes or until tops are a pale golden
color and inserted knife pulls out clean. Remove cupcakes and
place on a rack to cool.

To prepare frosting combine cream cheese, butter, vanilla,
lemon zest and juice in a medium mixing bowl. Beat ingredients with an electric mixer until light and fluffy. Gradually beat
in sugar. Cover and refrigerate. Once cupcakes are cool and
frosting is firm, frost cupcakes.

Makes 12 cupcakes

Huckleberry Pie with Lattice Crust

Serve with vanilla or Huckleberry Ice Cream (pg. 86).
Simply perfection.

Crust

2 cups all-purpose flour

½ teaspoon salt

12 tablespoons (1½ sticks) unsalted butter, chilled
and cut into ½-inch cubes

3 tablespoons vegetable shortening, chilled and cut
into ½-inch cubes

¼ cup ice water

Pie Filling

4½ cups (2 pints) huckleberries

¾ cup sugar

¼ cup all-purpose flour

2 tablespoons lemon juice

2 teaspoons freshly grated lemon zest

1 teaspoon vanilla extract

Egg Wash
1 egg
½ cup heavy cream

In a large mixing bowl, combine flour and salt. Add the butter and shortening. Using a pastry cutter or fingertips, work butter into flour until mixture resembles coarse meal. Very gradually add the ice water bit by bit working the dough as little as possible and adding as little water as possible until the pastry is formed into a ball. Wrap and chill for at least 1 hour.

When ready to assemble pie, place oven rack in lower third of oven and preheat to 400°F. Combine all pie-filling ingredients in a large bowl and mix thoroughly. Let stand for about 15 minutes. Prepare egg wash by whisking egg and cream together.

Transfer half of the dough onto a lightly floured work surface. Roll out to a 12½-inch round. Brush with egg wash and place in a 9-inch-diameter pie dish, egg wash side down. Pour huckleberry filling into crust.

Roll out second piecrust on lightly floured surface to 12-inch round. Cut dough into generous ½-inch-wide strips. Arrange dough strips horizontally across top of filling, spacing evenly apart. Form lattice by weaving remaining strips vertically. Trim dough strips even with overhang on bottom crust. Press dough strips and overhand together to seal and crimp edges. Brush crust with egg wash.

Place pie on baking sheet to catch any overflow. Bake for 50 minutes or until pie filling bubbles thickly in center. Cool before serving.

Serves 8

Huckleberry Sorbet

4 cups huckleberries
2 cups sugar
2 cups water
3 tablespoons lemon juice

Place all ingredients into a blender. Blend until smooth. Pour mixture into a fine-mesh wire strainer placed over a bowl. Place in refrigerator to strain and cool, about 3 hours.

Pour mixture into an ice-cream machine and process according to the manufacturer's instructions. Transfer to an airtight container and freeze until ready to serve.

Makes about 4 cups

Huckleberry Ice Cream

2 cups huckleberries
¾ cup sugar
⅛ teaspoon salt
1 cup milk
1½ cups heavy cream

Place huckleberries, sugar, salt, and milk in a blender. Blend until smooth. Stir in cream. Pour mixture into a fine-mesh wire strainer placed over a bowl. Place in refrigerator to strain and cool, about 3 hours.

Pour mixture into an ice-cream machine and process according to the manufacturer's instructions. Transfer to an airtight container and freeze until ready to serve.

Makes about 4 cups

HUCKLEBERRY CAPITAL OF THE WORLD

In 1981, the Montana State Legislature officially proclaimed Trout Creek, Montana, the "Huckleberry Capital of the World." A small town in the northwest part of the state, Trout Creek is famous for its abundance of the purple berry and home to the premier huckleberry festival in the West. Visitors from far and near flock to the town to eat and celebrate the juicy berry that embodies the spirit of the region. Festival activities include a 5-K run, huckleberry pancake breakfast, parade, and the grand huckleberry festival auction to name just a few. The weekend's activities culminate in arguably everyone's favorite event—the huckleberry dessert contest. Always the second weekend in August 2009 will mark the festival's thirtieth year.

HUCKLEBERRY BUNDT CAKE

The addition of huckleberries to this basic bundt cake
enhances this favorite classic cake.

3 cups all purpose flour
1 tablespoon baking powder
1 teaspoon salt
1⅔ cups sugar
¾ cup (1½ sticks) unsalted butter, room temperature
3 large eggs
2 teaspoons vanilla extract
1 cup buttermilk
1½ cups frozen huckleberries
Huckleberry Glaze (pg. 99)
Powdered sugar

Tip: *Use frozen berries to keep the huckleberries from sinking*
to the bottom of the cake as it bakes.

Preheat oven to 350°F. Prepare a 10-inch-diameter bundt pan with cooking spray or butter and flour. Whisk flour, baking powder, and salt in medium bowl. Using electric mixer, beat sugar and butter in a separate bowl. Beat in eggs and vanilla. Add dry ingredients in batches alternating with buttermilk. Fold in huckleberries.

Pour batter into a prepared pan. Bake on center rack in oven for 50 to 60 minutes or until inserted knife pulls out clean. Remove from oven and cool in pan. Transfer cake to serving plate and dust with powdered sugar.

Makes 10–12 servings

Chocolate Torte with Huckleberry Filling and Ganache

True chocoholics and huckleberry lovers alike will relish in this rich, dense, and decadent dessert.

Cake
8-1 ounce squares (1 package) semi-sweet chocolate
¾ cup unsalted butter, cut into ½-inch cubes
½ cup sugar
2 teaspoons vanilla
5 eggs, separated
¼ cup all-purposed flour
Dash of cream of tartar
Dash of salt

Filling
1 cup Huckleberry Jam (pg. 98)

Ganache
¾ cup heavy cream
2 tablespoons unsalted butter
8 ounces bittersweet chocolate, chopped

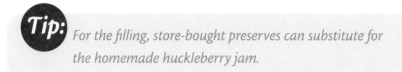

Tip: *For the filling, store-bought preserves can substitute for the homemade huckleberry jam.*

Preheat oven to 325°F. Prepare a 9½-inch springform cake pan with cooking spray or butter and flour.

In a large saucepan combine the chocolate, butter, and sugar. Cook over moderate heat until the chocolate and butter have melted, and the sugar has dissolved. Remove from heat and stir in vanilla. Let stand for 10 minutes.

Once cool, whisk the egg yolks into the chocolate mixture one at a time, beating well after each addition. Stir in the flour.

In a separate large bowl beat the egg whites until foamy. Add cream of tartar and salt. Beat until stiff peaks are formed. Whisk ⅓ of the egg whites into the chocolate mixture. Carefully stir in the remaining whites. Pour batter into prepared pan. Bake on center rack in oven for 45 to 60 minutes or until inserted knife pulls out clean. Remove from oven and transfer cake to a wire cooling rack. Carefully remove sides of the springform pan. Cool completely, and then gently remove the base.

To prepare ganache heat the cream and butter in a heavy saucepan over medium heat. Bring just to a boil. Remove from heat and whisk in chocolate. Let cool, stirring occasionally, until thickened but still pourable.

To assemble, carefully cut cake in half horizontally. Cover bottom cake layer with Huckleberry Jam and replace top layer. Pour ganache over cake. Use a rubber spatula to smooth ganache over top and sides until evenly coated. Let stand about 1 hour before serving. Dust with powdered sugar for a polished presentation.

Serves 12–16

Vanilla Bean Cheesecake with Huckleberry Glaze

This classic cheesecake is enhanced by fresh vanilla and huckleberries.

Crust
2⅓ cups graham cracker crumbs
½ cup (1 stick) unsalted butter, melted
¼ cup sugar

Cheesecake
2 vanilla beans split lengthwise
1/3 cup whipping cream
3 8-ounce packages cream cheese, room temperature
1 cup sugar
½ cup sour cream
2 teaspoons vanilla extract
4 large eggs

Topping
Huckleberry Glaze (pg. 99)

Preheat oven to 375°F. Wrap the outside of a 10-inch-diameter springform pan with aluminum foil. In a mixing bowl combine all crust ingredients. Using a pasty cutter, fingertips, or food processor blend until moist crumbs are formed. Press mixture firmly onto bottom and sides of prepared pan. Bake on center rack in oven for 10 minutes or until crust begins to brown. Transfer crust in pan to rack and cool. Maintain oven temperature while preparing cheesecake filling.

Split vanilla beans. Scrape the seeds into a heavy saucepan over medium heat. Add beans and cream and bring to a boil. Immediately remove from heat and cool completely. Strain mixture through a fine-wire strainer and discard beans. Set aside.

Using an electric mixer, beat cream cheese and sugar in a large bowl for several minutes until smooth. Add vanilla-cream mixture, sour cream, and vanilla. Beat until well blended. One at a time beat in the eggs. Pour filling into prepared crust. Bake for about one hour. Cake should be golden and beginning to crack around edges. Cool completely and remove from pan. Top with huckleberry glaze.

Serves 8–12

Staples

Huckleberry Coulis

Drizzle this sauce over cheesecake, ice cream, waffles, pancakes, or any dish needing some extra pizzazz. This is also our basic syrup recipe.

1½ cups huckleberries
¼ cup sugar
1 teaspoon lemon juice
1 teaspoon vanilla extract (or almond extract)

Place huckleberries in blender or food processor and puree. In a heavy saucepan combine the puree, sugar, lemon juice, and vanilla extract. Simmer on moderately low heat, stirring occasionally for about 10 minutes. Remove from heat and strain through a fine-mesh wire sieve. Transfer mixture to a bowl or squeeze bottle and chill until completely cooled and ready to serve.

Makes about 1½ cups

HUCKLEBERRY COMPOTE

More substantial than a coulis or glaze, compote is less of an accent and more of a hearty topping.

2½ cups huckleberries
⅓ cup sugar
⅓ cup water
1 teaspoon cinnamon
1 teaspoon cloves
1 teaspoon nutmeg

In heavy saucepan combine 1½ cups berries, sugar, water, and spices. Simmer over medium heat until berries burst, stirring often, about 10 minutes. Add remaining 1 cup berries. Continue stirring and cook until mixture coats spoon, about 10 minutes. Serve warm.

Makes about 2 cups

HUCKLEBERRY JAM

This freezer jam is quick and easy to prepare and delicious on fresh bread.

4½ cups fresh huckleberries, crushed
5 cups sugar
6 ounces liquid fruit pectin
2 tablespoons lemon juice

In a large bowl combine crushed berries and sugar. Mix thoroughly. Let stand for 10 minutes. Add liquid pectin and lemon juice. Stir continuously for 3 minutes. Pour jam into freezer containers leaving ½-inch gap at top for expansion. Place in refrigerator and let stand until jam sets, about 3 hours. Serve or transfer to freezer. Fresh jam can be refrigerated up to 3 weeks.

Makes 7 cups (3½ pints)

HUCKLEBERRY GLAZE

A wonderful garnish for desserts, this glaze can also be applied to baked ham.

2 cups huckleberries
½ cup water
1 tablespoon sugar
2 teaspoons cornstarch

In heavy saucepan combine all ingredients. Over medium heat bring mixture to a boil. Stir continuously for 1 minute. Remove from heat and cool slightly.

Makes 2 cups

Huckleberry Barbeque Sauce

From fish to fowl, try this sauce on anything that needs an extra kick.

2 – 14½ ounce cans diced tomatoes

1 tablespoon tomato paste

1 tablespoon apple cider vinegar

1 teaspoon balsamic vinegar

2 teaspoons Worcestershire sauce

1 tablespoon molasses

½ cup brown sugar

3 tablespoon huckleberry preserves

1 jalapeño, seeded and chopped

½ bell pepper

4 cloves garlic, chopped

1 teaspoon granulated onion

1 teaspoon dry mustard

1 teaspoon fresh ground black pepper

1 teaspoon sea salt

1 pinch crushed red pepper (optional)

In medium saucepan add tomatoes, tomato paste, vinegars, and Worcestershire sauce. Bring to a boil. Reduce heat and simmer 15 minutes. Add remaining ingredients and simmer another 15 minutes. Set aside to cool. Use blender or food processor to puree sauce.

Makes about 3 cups

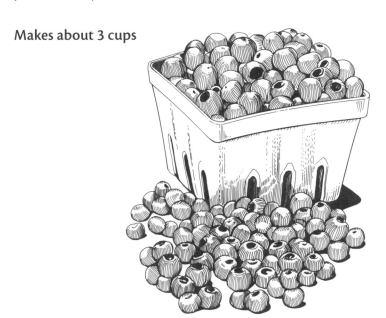

Huckleberry Vinaigrette

¼ cup huckleberry vinegar

½ cup olive oil

2 tablespoons huckleberry preserves

¾ cup walnuts, chopped

½ teaspoon salt

¼ teaspoon freshly ground pepper

In a small mixing bowl whisk together vinegar, oil, and huckleberry preserves. Add walnuts, salt, and pepper. Whisk dressing until well blended.

Makes 1½ cups

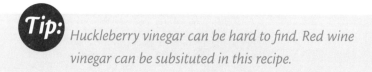

Tip: *Huckleberry vinegar can be hard to find. Red wine vinegar can be subsituted in this recipe.*

HUCKLEBERRY MARINADE

Use to marinate fish, poultry, pork, and vegetables or use as a simple salad dressing.

   ¼ cup huckleberries
   ¼ cup red wine vinegar
   ½ cup olive oil
   Salt and pepper to taste

Place all ingredients in a blender and puree.

Makes 1 cup

Huckleberry Chutney

A savory-sweet blend, this chutney is a good relish for grilled pork or roast turkey.

1 cup huckleberries
½ cup apple juice
2 tablespoons onions, diced
1½ tablespoons fresh ginger root, grated
¼ cup brown sugar, packed
2 tablespoons cider vinegar (or red wine vinegar)
1½ tablespoons corn starch
⅛ tablespoon salt
1 pinch cinnamon
1 pinch nutmeg
½ teaspoon crushed red pepper (optional)

Combine all ingredients in a large saucepan. Bring to a boil over medium heat. Stirring continuously for 1 minute. Cover and refrigerate 30–45 minutes.

Makes 1½ cups

Huckleberry Cream Cheese Spread

A wonderful spread on your favorite bagel.

8 ounces light cream cheese
⅓ cup fresh huckleberries or 1 tablespoon preserves

Use a mixer or food process and blend thoroughly. Refrigerate until used.

Makes 1 cup

Huckleberry Horseradish Sauce

This sauce can be used with everything from prime rib to po' boys.

¼ cup prepared horseradish
¼ cup mayonnaise
¼ cup sour cream
1 tablespoon Dijon mustard
1 tablespoon huckleberry preserves

Blend all ingredients in blender or food processor until smooth. Refrigerate until used.

Makes 1 cup

HUCKLEBERRY FESTIVALS

During huckleberry season there is an abundance of festivals throughout the Rocky Mountains and Pacific Northwest (and beyond, some in surprising places) to celebrate and indulge in the berry sometimes called the "purple gem." These annual events include a multitude of events from pancake breakfasts to pie-eating contests to bake-offs and music to arts and crafts and even a Miss Huckleberry Pageant. Typically these festivals occur in August (note exceptions). Check with the local chamber of commerce for exact dates and locations.

Huckleberry Festival
Donnelly, Idaho

Huckleberry Festival
Priest Lake, Idaho

Potato/Huckleberry Festival (September)
Rexburg, Idaho

Huckleberry Heritage Festival
Wallace, Idaho (3rd weekend in August)

Huckleberry Festival (September)
Bingen, Oregon

Blue Mountain Huckleberry Festival (July)
North Powder, Oregon

The Mount Hood Huckleberry Festival & Barlow
*   Trail Days*
Welches, Oregon

The Swan Lake Huckleberry Festival
Swan Lake, Montana

Huckleberry Festival
Trout Creek, Montana (2nd weekend in August)
(www.huckleberryfestival.com)

Huckleberry Days Art Festival
Whitefish, Montana

Huckleberry Hustle and Festival (July)
Flint, Michigan

Shawangunk Mountain Wild Blueberry &
    Huckleberry Festival
Ellenville, New York

Castle Mountain Huckleberry Festival
Pincher Creek, Alberta

RESOURCES

Bowen, 'Asta. *The Huckleberry Book.* Helena, Mont.:
American Geographic Publishing, 1988.

Krumm, Bob. *The Rocky Mountain Berry Book.* Helena, Mont.:
Falcon Publishing, 1991.

Richards, Rebecca T. and Susan J. Alexander. "A Social History
of Wild Huckleberry Harvesting in the Pacific Northwest."
General Technical Report PNW-GTR-657. Portland, Oreg.:
U.S. Department of Agriculture, Forest Service, Pacific
Northwest Research Station.

INDEX

ABOUT THE AUTHORS

Alex and Stephanie Hester have lived in huckleberry country for most of their lives. Near their family cabin in Montana, they have their own secret picking spot where they have spent many hours hand-picking berries and using them to prepare delicious dishes. Both Alex and Stephanie earned their undergraduate degrees in Environmental Studies from The Evergreen State College in Olympia, Washington. Alex is a counselor and supervisor at a residential treatment center for children by day. In his spare time, he caters special events and private parties and enjoys experimenting in the kitchen. Stephanie recently completed an M.B.A. program at the University of Montana in Missoula, and she works for the National Parks Conservation Association. She enjoys eating Alex's dishes, spending time in the outdoors, and traveling. Stephanie and Alex reside in Helena, Montana, with their son, Jack.